A WINNING SKILLS BOOK

You Can Be Creative!

Joy Berry

Illustrated by Bartholomew

Joy Berry Enterprises

Copyright © Joy Berry, 2022
Originally Published 2013

All rights are reserved.

No part of this book can be duplicated or used without the prior written permission of the copyright owner, except for the use of brief quotations from the book.

For inquiries or permission requests contact the publisher.

Published by Joy Berry Enterprises
www.joyberryenterprises.com

Joy Berry Enterprises

You can be creative if you know about
- the definition of creativity,
- concrete creations,
- abstract creations,
- the inherent value of creations,
- skills, talents, and gifts, and
- discovering and utilizing gifts.

THE DEFINITION OF CREATIVITY

To create is to bring into existence something that did not exist before.

Creativity is the ability to create. Creativity is a characteristic that is inherent in all human beings. Every person has the potential to create and, therefore, is creative.

THE DEFINITION OF CREATIVITY

A creation is something that has been created.

THE DEFINITION OF CREATIVITY   7

Creating is a unique process that is as important as the creation it produces. What happens to a creator while he or she is creating is as important as whatever is created.

CONCRETE CREATIONS

Some creations are **concrete**.

Concrete creations are ones that are experienced with the five senses.

Some concrete creations can be looked at.

Other concrete creations can be listened to.

Some concrete creations can be tasted.

Other concrete creations can be smelled.

Some concrete creations can be touched and felt.

Other concrete creations can be useful.

ABSTRACT CREATIONS

Some creations are **abstract**.

Abstract creations are ones that can be experienced mentally and emotionally.

Some abstract creations cause people to think.

Other abstract creations cause people to experience emotions.

ABSTRACT CREATIONS

Some abstract creations provide a sense of worth and well being.

Other abstract creations provide a sense of belonging.

ABSTRACT CREATIONS

Some abstract creations motivate people to do things.

Other abstract creations create solutions to problems.

ABSTRACT CREATIONS

Some abstract creations create order.

Other abstract creations create a system or program.

THE INHERENT VALUE OF CREATING

Because every human being is unique, every person is uniquely creative and, therefore, produces creations that are not like any other person's creations.

Because every creation is unique, it cannot be compared to other creations to determine whether it is good or bad.

THE INHERENT VALUE OF CREATING

Although other people can judge a person's creation and decide whether they like it, their judgment does not make the creation good or bad.

A creator is the only person who can determine whether his or her creation is good or bad. A creator determines this by deciding whether the creation accomplishes whatever it was designed to accomplish.

26 SKILLS, TALENTS, AND GIFTS

Skills, talents, and gifts are used to create both concrete and abstract creations.

A **skill** is an ability to do something.

A skill needs to be practiced before it can be developed as well as possible.

SKILLS, TALENTS, AND GIFTS

A **talent** is a skill that a person has the potential to do very well.

Talents **cannot** be acquired. People are born with them.

SKILLS, TALENTS, AND GIFTS

A **gift** is a talent that is accompanied by an intense desire to use it.

Gifts **cannot** be acquired. People are born with them. Every person is born with one or more gifts. Therefore, **every person is gifted.**

Important creations come into existence when people use their gifts. Therefore, people are most effectively creative when they discover and utilize their gifts.

Since gifts are accompanied by an intense desire to use them, people who do not use their gifts can become extremely frustrated and unhappy.

To avoid frustration caused by not using a gift, it is necessary to discover and use your gifts.

DISCOVERING AND UTILIZING GIFTS

You can discover your gifts by taking a **personal inventory**. To do this, make four lists.

On List #1, list the things you think you do best.

On List #2, list the things you most enjoy doing or enjoy the results of doing.

Be sure that you do not confuse enjoyment with fun. Fun is often times frivolous and provides momentary pleasure. However, enjoyment provides genuine positive feelings and a sense of satisfaction that can last a long time.

On List #3, list the things you are most motivated to do. This can include things you have an intense desire to do now. It can also include things you have an intense desire to do in the future.

DISCOVERING AND UTILIZING GIFTS 37

On List #4, list the things you do or want to do that can produce meaningful and rewarding results. This includes anything that enhances
- your life,
- the lives of other people, and/or
- the world in which you live.

Once you have completed all four lists, compare them and circle those things that appear on all four lists.

The things that appear on all four lists are your gifts.

Some people have only one gift; other people have more than one. How many gifts a person has is **not** what is important. What **is** important is how effectively a person uses whatever gifts he or she has.

Once you have taken a personal inventory, it is a good idea to validate your results. You can do this by talking to family members and close friends who know you well.

Before sharing the results of your inventory, ask these people to tell you what they think are your gifts. It is possible that they might come up with things you did not think of.

Next, share you personal inventory with your family members and close friends. Get their responses to your conclusions.

Evaluate their responses. Then decide whether you want to incorporate their responses into the process of discovering your gifts.

Another way to validate the results of you personal inventory is to talk with a professional counselor. This could be someone such as a school counselor or a career counselor.

You can also take an aptitude or career test. These are available at
- your school,
- your community college, and/or
- a career counselor's office.

Once you have discovered your gifts, it is essential to begin developing and using them immediately.

Not developing and using your gifts can cause you to become frustrated and unhappy. This can cause you to misbehave and possibly get yourself into trouble.

Not developing and using your gifts can also rob others of the contributions your gifts were intended to produce.

This can cause others to feel resentful toward you.

Once you discover your gifts, it is imperative to find ways you can use your gifts in the future.

Then you need to do whatever is necessary to prepare yourself to use your gifts to the fullest.

People are given gifts so they can make some kind of contribution to the world in which they live.

People who do not use their gifts miss out on the opportunity to make the contributions they were born to make.

48 CONCLUSION

To make the most out of your life, discover and use whatever gifts you have!

www.ingramcontent.com/pod-product-compliance
Lightning Source LLC
Chambersburg PA
CBHW081408070526
44583CB00020B/2725